Get rich with cryptocurrencies

Paul Mihalache

ISBN: **197657756X**
ISBN-13: **978-1976577567**

DEDICATION

This book is dedicated to the Modern-Renaissance man. An outstandingly versatile, well-rounded person. The expression alludes to such Renaissance figures as Leonardo da Vinci, who performed brilliantly in many different fields. I hope this book will give you enough information to become wealthier and have a happier life.

CONTENTS

Acknowledgments

1 WHAT IS A CRYPTOCURRENCY Pg 9

2 CRYPTOCURRENCIES Pg 12

3 HOW I INVESTED Pg 25

4 INVESTMENT TIME Pg #

5 FAUCET Pg #

6 MINING Pg

VOCABULARY Pg #

ACKNOWLEDGMENTS

A cryptocurrency is a digital asset designed to work as a medium of exchange using cryptography to secure the transactions and to control the creation of additional units of the currency.

Cryptocurrencies are classified as a subset of digital currencies and are also classified as a subset of alternative and virtual currencies.

Bitcoin became the first decentralized cryptocurrency in 2009.

Since then, numerous cryptocurrencies have been created. The decentralized control is related to the use of bitcoin's blockchain transaction database in the role of a distributed ledger.

* This content is for information and educational purposes only and should not be considered investment advice or an investment recommendation. Past performance is not an indication of future results. All trading involves risk. Only risk capital you're prepared to lose.

1 . WHAT IS A CRYPTOCURRENCY

In December 2014 , my brother told about a virtual coin with great prospect to be the future currency of the world. I laughed so hard but I listened to his story. Was a bit of a fairy tale to believe that a virtual coin can be the future in global economy but I made a note in my mind and I did a bit of research.

Bitcoin was the name of this currency and it was invented by an unknown programmer, or a group of programmers, under the name Satoshi Nakamoto and released as open-source software in 2009. The system is peer-to-peer, and transactions take place between users directly, without an intermediary. These transactions are verified by network nodes and recorded in a public distributed ledger called a blockchain. The value of a bitcoin in December 2014 was £250 and I was still sceptic to invest in something that I have so little knowledge. The value decreased a lot over the new year and I decided to invest a few bucks. I bought 1 Bitcoin in January 2015 at a value of £155. In August I spent £65 to buy a bit more than a half of Bitcoin.

In October 2015 I was happy to sell my 1.6 Bitcoins for £320. I made a small profit of £100 without any effort. By then I had no clue how much I would regret selling. I checked the value of the Bitcoin a minute ago to be shocked : £3511.83 (£3042.30 more than last year). At today value, the 1.6 bitcoin I sold in 2015 will be £5619, generating a 2554% profit.

I just hope with the knowledge from this book and sharing my experience will help you to avoid the school boy error I did at the beginning of my cryptocurrencies investments.

	Received bitcoin from CoinPot	0.00026733 £0.72

October 2015

	Sold bitcoin using EUR Wallet	-1.60077582 -£311.75

August 2015

	Received bitcoin from Bitcoin address	0.44588827 £64.18

	Bought bitcoin using EUR Wallet	1.15400755 £176.02

June 2015

	Sold bitcoin using EUR Wallet	-1.1...3

9

By now the first question in your head will be "What is a cryptocurrency?"

A cryptocurrency is a digital asset designed to work as a medium of exchange using cryptography to secure the transactions and to control the creation of additional units of the currency. Cryptocurrencies are classified as a subset of digital currencies and are also classified as a subset of alternative currencies and virtual currencies.

Bitcoin became the first decentralized cryptocurrency in 2009. Since then, numerous cryptocurrencies have been created. These are frequently called altcoins, as a blend of bitcoin alternative. Bitcoin and its derivatives use decentralized control as opposed to centralized electronic money/centralized banking systems. The decentralized control is related to the use of bitcoin's blockchain transaction database in the role of a distributed ledger.

Decentralized cryptocurrency is produced by the entire cryptocurrency system collectively, at a rate which is defined when the system is created and which is publicly known. In case of decentralized cryptocurrency, companies or governments cannot produce new units, and have not so far provided backing for other firms, banks or corporate entities which hold asset value measured in it. The underlying technical system upon which decentralized cryptocurrencies are based was created by the group or individual known as Satoshi Nakamoto.

As of March 2015, hundreds of cryptocurrency specifications exist, most are similar to and derived from the first fully implemented decentralized cryptocurrency, bitcoin. Within cryptocurrency systems the safety, integrity and balance of ledgers is maintained by a community of mutually distrustful parties referred to as miners: members of the general public using their computers to help validate and timestamp transactions adding them to the ledger in accordance with a particular timestamping scheme. The security of cryptocurrency ledgers is based on the assumption that the majority of miners are honestly trying to maintain the ledger, having financial incentive to do so.

Most cryptocurrencies are designed to gradually decrease production of currency, placing an ultimate cap on the total amount of currency that will ever be in circulation, mimicking precious metals. Compared with ordinary currencies held by financial institutions or kept as cash on hand, cryptocurrencies can be more difficult for seizure by law enforcement.

This difficulty is derived from leveraging cryptographic technologies.

The legal status of cryptocurrencies varies substantially from country to country and is still undefined or changing in many of them. While some countries have explicitly allowed their use and trade, others have banned or restricted it. Likewise, various government agencies, departments, and courts have classified bitcoins differently.

China Central Bank banned the handling of bitcoins by financial institutions in China during an extremely fast adoption period in early 2014. In Russia, though cryptocurrencies are legal, it is illegal to actually purchase goods with any currency other than the Russian ruble.

On March 25, 2014, the United States Internal Revenue Service (IRS) ruled that bitcoin will be treated as property for tax purposes as opposed to currency. This means bitcoin will be subject to capital gains tax. One benefit of this ruling is that it clarifies the legality of bitcoin. No longer do investors need to worry that investments in or profit made from bitcoins are illegal or how to report them to the IRS.

In a paper published by researchers from Oxford and Warwick, it was shown that bitcoin has some characteristics more like the precious metals market than traditional currencies, hence in agreement with the IRS decision even if based on different reasons.

As the popularity of and demand for online currencies increases since the inception of bitcoin in 2009, so do concerns that such an unregulated person to person global economy that cryptocurrencies offer may become a threat to society. Concerns abound that altcoins may become tools for anonymous web criminals.

Cryptocurrency networks display a marked lack of regulation that attracts many users who seek decentralized exchange and use of currency; however the very same lack of regulations has been critiqued as potentially enabling criminals who seek to evade taxes and launder money.

Transactions that occur through the use and exchange of these altcoins are independent from formal banking systems, and therefore can make tax evasion simpler for individuals. Since charting taxable income is based upon what a recipient reports to the revenue service, it becomes extremely difficult to account for transactions made using existing cryptocurrencies, a mode of exchange that is complex and (in some cases) impossible to track.

Systems of anonymity that most cryptocurrencies offer can also serve as a simpler means to launder money. Rather than laundering money through an intricate net of financial actors and offshore bank accounts, laundering money through altcoins stands outside institutions and can be achieved through anonymous transactions. Laundering services for cryptocurrency exist to service the bitcoin currency, in which multiple sourced bitcoins are blended to obscure the relationship between input and output addresses.

2 CRYPTOCURRENCIES

Since December 2014, when I had my first contact with cryptocurrencies, I started to read more about them, to study and to develop a growing interest in how to invest and gain money from cryptocurrencies.

There were more than 900 cryptocurrencies available over the internet as of 11 July 2017 and growing. New cryptocurrency can be created any time. By market capitalization, Bitcoin is currently the largest blockchain network, followed by Ethereum, Bitcoin Cash, Ripple and Litecoin.

Here is a list of the most important cryptocurrencies, with release year, name, symbol, founder and notes:

2014	Auroracoin	AUR	Baldur Odinsson (pseudonym)	Created as an alternative to fiat currency in Iceland.
2009	Bitcoin	BTC	Satoshi Nakamoto	The first decentralized ledger currency. Cryptocurrency with the most famous, popular, notable and highest market capitalization.
2017	Bitcoin Cash	BCH		Hard fork from Bitcoin
2017	BitConnect	BCC		The community driven decentralized cryptocurrency that allow people to store and invest their wealth in a non-government controlled currency, and even earn a substantial interest.

2014	BlackCoin	BC	Rat4 (pseudonym)	Secures its network through a process called minting.
2014	Burstcoin	BURST	Burstcoin Community	First Proof of Capacity coin, First Smart Contract, First Atomic Cross Chain Transfer.
2014	Coinye	KOI, COYE		Used American hip hop artist Kanye West as its mascot, abandoned after trademark lawsuit.
2014[11]	Dash	DASH	Evan Duffield & Kyle Hagan	A bitcoin-based currency featuring instant transactions, decentralized governance and budgeting, and private transactions.
2013	Dogecoin	DOGE, XDG	Jackson Palmer & Billy Markus	Based on an internet meme.
2014	DigitalNote	XDN	XDN-dev team, dNote	A private cryptocurrency with an instant untraceable crypto messages and first blockchain banking implementation, use CryptoNote protocol.
2013	Emercoin	EMC	EvgenijM86 & Yitshak Dorfman	Trusted storage for any small data: acts as an alternative, decentralized DNS, PKI store, SSL infrastructure and other.

2015	Ethereum	ETH	Vitalik Buterin	Supports Turing-complete smart contracts.
2015	Ethereum Classic	ETC		An alternative version of Ethereum[20] whose blockchain does not include the DAO Hard-fork.[21][22] Supports Turing-complete smart contracts.
2013	Gridcoin	GRC	Rob Hälford	The first cryptocurrency linked to citizen science through the Berkeley Open Infrastructure for Network Computing
2015	IOTA	IOT, MIOT	...	The first cryptocurrency using the Tangle, a next generation blockchain, as distributed ledger technology.
2011	Litecoin	LTC	Charles Lee	The first cryptocurrency to use Scrypt as a hashing algorithm.
2014	MazaCoin	MZC	BTC Oyate Initiative	The underlying software is derived from that of another cryptocurrency, ZetaCoin.
2014	Monero	XMR	Monero Core Team	Privacy-centric coin using the CryptoNote protocol with improvements for scalability and decentralization.

2011	Namecoin	NMC	Vincent Durham	Also acts as an alternative, decentralized DNS.
2014	NEM	XEM	UtopianFuture (pseudonym)	The first hybrid public/private blockchain solution built from scratch, and first to use the Proof of Importance algorithm using EigenTrust++ reputation system.
2014	Nxt	NXT	BCNext (pseudonym)	Specifically designed as a flexible platform to build applications and financial services around its protocol.
2013	Omni	MSC	J. R. Willett	Omni is both digital currency and communications protocol built on top of the existing bitcoin block chain.
2012	Peercoin	PPC	Sunny King (pseudonym)	The first cryptocurrency to use POW and POS functions.
2014	PotCoin	POT		Developed to service the legalized cannabis industry
2013	Primecoin	XPM	Sunny King (pseudonym)	Uses the finding of prime chains composed of Cunningham chains and bi-twin chains for proof-of-work, which can lead to useful byproducts.

2013	Ripple	XRP	Chris Larsen & Jed McCaleb	Designed for peer to peer debt transfer. Not based on bitcoin.
2015	SixEleven	SIL	fflo (pseudonym)	Also acts as an alternative, decentralized DNS.
2011	SwiftCoin	STC	Daniel Bruno, Chartered Market Technician	First digital coin with theoretical value based on the work required to produce electricity. First block chain to support currency creation by interest paid on debt. Solidus Bond proto smart-contract. One of the first digital coins patented in the US. First block chain to support encrypted mail with attachments.
2014	Synereo AMP	AMP	Dor Konforty & Greg Meredith	Trying to create a world computer, Synereo's 2.0 tech stack incorporates all faculties needed to support decentralized computation without central servers.
2014	Titcoin	TIT	Edward Mansfield & Richard Allen	The first cryptocurrency to be nominated for a major adult industry award
2017	Ubiq	UBQ	Julian Yap	Supports Turing-complete smart contracts; air-gapped fork of Ethereum

2014	Vertcoin	VTC	Bushido	Next-gen ASIC resistance and first to implement stealth addresses.
2016	Zcash	ZEC	Zooko Wilcox	The first open, permission less financial system employing zero-knowledge security.

Bitcoin is a worldwide cryptocurrency and digital payment system called the first decentralized digital currency, since the system works without a central repository or single administrator. It was invented by an unknown programmer, or a group of programmers, under the name Satoshi Nakamoto and released as open-source software in 2009. The system is peer-to-peer, and transactions take place between users directly, without an intermediary. These transactions are verified by network nodes and recorded in a public distributed ledger called a blockchain. It has worldwide payments and zero or low processing fees.

Besides being created as a reward for mining, bitcoin can be exchanged for other currencies, products, and services. As of February 2015, over 100,000 merchants and vendors accepted bitcoin as payment. Bitcoin can also be held as an investment. According to research produced by Cambridge University in 2017, there are 2.9 to 5.8 million unique users using a cryptocurrency wallet, most of them using bitcoin. On 1 August 2017 bitcoin split into two derivative digital currencies, the classic bitcoin (BTC) and the Bitcoin Cash (BCH).

Bitcoin Cash is a spin off fork of Bitcoin. It is run by the Chinese and had a larger block size, so you can one day buy coffee with your Bitcoin. Bitcoin Cash is also known as BCH or BCC.

On July 20, 2017, the bitcoin miners voted, 97% in favor, on the Bitcoin Improvement Proposal (BIP) 91. The proposal, by Bitmain Warranty engineer James Hilliard, was to activate Segregated Witness (SegWit).

Some members of the bitcoin community felt that adopting BIP 91 without increasing the block-size limit would simply delay confronting the issue and that it favored people who wanted to treat bitcoin as a digital investment rather than as a transactional currency. They announced implementation of Bitcoin Cash as a hard fork for August 1. It inherited the transaction history of the bitcoin currency on that date, but all later transactions were separate.

On August 9th, it was 30% more profitable to mine on the original chain. Even though the fork allows for a higher block size, block generation was so sporadic that the original chain was 920 MB bigger than the chain of the fork, as of 9 August 2017. Due to several difficulty adjustments, the profitability of mining either chain has then switched repeatedly and as of 30 August 2017 around 1,500 more blocks were mined on the Bitcoin Cash chain than on the original one.

BitShares is powered by BitShares, an open source technology. It allows you to trade cryptoequities and bitassets. BitShares is a family of DACs that implement the business model of a bank and exchange. BitShares offers a bank account where funds can be transferred in seconds anywhere in the world with more privacy and security than a Swiss bank account and the account can never be frozen, funds cannot be seized, and the bank can never face collapse. Unlike existing banks, account balance can be denominated in etc, silver, oil, or other commodities in addition to national currencies.

BitShares also serves as an exchange where currencies, commodities, and stock derivatives can be traded including shorts and options. The bank takes a cut on every transaction and pays these transaction fees to the delegates and then shareholders by way of the Burn Rate.

CureCoin is a CryptoCurrency based on coupling SHA-256 Mining and Folding@Home Protein Folding. This means you can help cure cancer and a number of other diseases by mining this coin! It's new and has great growth potential. CureCoin is also known as CURE.

Dash was initially released as XCoin, then known as DarkCoin.
Dash is a cryptocurrency aimed at bringing privacy back to transactions. This is something the Dash community feels Bitcoin has lost. Dash changed its name so as to distance itself from the growing notoriety of the DarkWeb. Dash uses Darksend as a method of achieving privacy in transactions. For this, it uses Masternodes. These are similar to Bitcoin tumblers, in a way. Transactions are all sent to a Masternode. Identical inputs are all into one transaction with various outgoing transactions. This process can be done multiple times to increase the obfuscation of the transactions.
Dash uses a two-tier architecture to power its network. The first tier consists of miners who secure the network and write transactions to the blockchain. The second tier consists of masternodes which enable the advanced features of Dash. Dash is near-instant due to the InstantX service. This is a service that allows one to lock inputs to only specific transactions and verify through consensus.

If consensus cannot be reached, the transaction falls back on standard verification. This process also allows Dash to solve the double spending problem without the long wait times of Bitcoin.

Dogecoin is a cryptocurrency featuring a likeness of the Shiba Inu dog from the "Doge" Internet meme as its logo. Introduced as a "joke currency" on 8 December 2013, Dogecoin quickly developed its own online community and reached a capitalization of US$60 million in January 2014; as of June 2017, it has a capitalization of US$340 million.

Compared with other cryptocurrencies, Dogecoin has a fast initial coin production schedule: 100 billion coins have been in circulation by mid-2015 with an additional 5.256 billion coins every year thereafter. As of 30 June 2015, the 100 billionth Dogecoin has been mined. While there are few mainstream commercial applications, the currency has gained traction as an Internet tipping system, in which social media users grant Dogecoin tips to other users for providing interesting or noteworthy content. Many members of the Dogecoin community, as well as members of other cryptocurrency communities, use the phrase "To the moon!" to describe the overall sentiment of the coin's rising value. Thanks to crowdfunding efforts, a gold coin representing the cryptocurrency is scheduled to reach the Moon's surface in 2019.

Dogecoin was intended to be fast, light, cheap, and easy to use. It was intended to reach a broader audience than Bitcoin, as well as separate a cryptocurrency from Bitcoin's shady past

Ethereum is a decentralized platform that runs smart contracts : applications that run exactly as programmed without any possibility of downtime, censorship, fraud or third party interference. Ethereum is how the Internet was supposed to work.

Ethereum was crowdfunded during August 2014 by fans all around the world. It is developed by ETHDEV with contributions from great minds across the globe.

Ethereum is an open-source, public, blockchain-based distributed computing platform featuring smart contract functionality. It provides a decentralized Turing-complete virtual machine, the Ethereum Virtual Machine (EVM), which can execute scripts using an international network of public nodes. Ethereum also provides a cryptocurrency token called "ether", which can be transferred between accounts and used to compensate participant nodes for computations performed.

Ethereum was proposed in late 2013 by Vitalik Buterin, a cryptocurrency researcher and programmer. Development was funded by an online crowdsale during July–August 2014. The system went live on 30 July 2015.

In 2016 Ethereum was forked into two blockchains, as a result of the collapse of The DAO project, thereby creating Ethereum Classic.

Ethereum Classic is the original chain of Ethereum. Ethereum Classic is a decentralized platform that runs smart contracts: applications that run exactly as programmed without any possibility of downtime, censorship, fraud or third party interference.

Ethereum Classic is a continuation of the original Ethereum blockchain - the classic version preserving untampered history; free from external interference and subjective tampering of transactions.

Ethereum Classic appeared as a result of disagreement with the Ethereum Foundation regarding The DAO Hard Fork. It united members of the Ethereum community who rejected the hard fork on philosophical grounds. Users that owned ETH before the DAO hard fork (1900000th block) received the same amount of ETC after the fork.

Ethereum Classic passed a technical hard fork to adjust the internal prices for various opcodes of the Ethereum Virtual Machine (EVM) on October 25, 2016, similar to the hard fork committed by Ethereum a week previously. The purpose of the hard fork was a more rational distribution of payments for resource-intensive calculations, which led to the elimination of the favorable conditions for attacks that were previously conducted on ETH and ETC. A hard fork held in the beginning of 2017 successfully delayed the "bomb complexity" that was added to the Ethereum code in September 2015 with a view of exponentially increasing the complexity of mining and the process of calculation of new network units. The next hard fork is scheduled for late 2017 with the aim of changing the monetary policy with unlimited emissions to a system similar to Bitcoin.

Golem is a global, open sourced, decentralized supercomputer that anyone can access. It's made up of the combined power of user's machines, from personal laptops to entire datacenters. Anyone will be able to use Golem to compute any program you can think of, from rendering to research to running websites, in a completely decentralized & inexpensive way. The Golem Network is a decentralized sharing economy of computing power, where anyone can make money 'renting' out their computing power or developing & selling software.

Gridcoin is a decentralized, open source math-based digital asset. It performs transactions peer-to-peer cryptographically without the need for a central issuing authority. It is the first block chain protocol that delivered a working algorithm that equally rewards and cryptographically proves solving BOINC hosted work, which can be virtually any kind of distributed computing process (ASIC/GPU/CPU/Sensor/Etc).

Gridcoin provides benefits to humanity through contributions to scientific research. It is the only crypto-currency that rewards individuals for BOINC contributions without the need for a central authority to distribute rewards.

Litecoin is the first Scrypt based cryptocurrency. Litecoin is by far and away the biggest market cap of the alt-coins. Litecoin provides faster transaction confirmations (2.5 minutes on average) and uses a memory-hard, scrypt-based mining proof-of-work algorithm to target the regular computers with GPUs most people already have. Litecoin is also known as LTC.

Creation and transfer of coins is based on an open source cryptographic protocol and is not managed by any central authority. While inspired by, and in most regards technically nearly identical to Bitcoin (BTC), Litecoin has some technical improvements over Bitcoin, and most other major cryptocurrencies, such as the adoption of Segregated Witness, and the Lightning Network. These effectively allow a greater number of transactions to be processed by the network in a given time, reducing potential bottlenecks, as seen with Bitcoin. Litecoin also has almost zero payment cost and facilitates payments approximately four times faster than Bitcoin.

MaidSafeCoin is also known as MAID. It has a good development team, with some interesting ideas behind it, such as farming to share your computer as a distributed Dropbox or Google Drive. The coin also has a large market cap, in the top 5.

MaidSafe aims to create a decentralized Internet, to be called the SAFE (Secure Access For Everyone) Network, by tapping unused computing resources to perform many of the tasks common to servers currently running the Internet. Safecoin is to be the credit system used by the SAFE Network. It will be issued to what they have named Farmers and Builders. Farmers are users of the MaidSafe client that will receive safecoin in exchange for running a node, committing their unused computer resources to the SAFE Network, such as storage space, CPU, and bandwidth. Builders are Open Source developers who will receive safecoin for building popular applications that utilize the SAFE Network.

Safecoin has a cap of 4.3 billion coins, of which only 10% have been released via this intermediary MaidSafeCoin. Despite only having 10% of the possible coins in circulation at this point, MaidSafeCoin hit the top 5 market cap in the cryptocurrency world .

Monero is a cryptocurrency that is a new privacy-centric coin using the CryptoNote protocol. It is gaining popularity recently, and a top 10 market cap coin. It's untraceable like DASH.

Unlike many cryptocurrencies that are derivatives of Bitcoin, Monero is based on the CryptoNote protocol and possesses significant algorithmic differences relating to blockchain obfuscation.

Monero experienced rapid growth in market capitalization (from US$5M to US$185M) and transaction volume during the year 2016, partly due to adoption in 2016 by major darknet market AlphaBay.

Monero is also known as XMR

Peercoin, also known as PPCoin or PPC, is a peer-to-peer cryptocurrency utilizing both proof-of-stake and proof-of-work systems.

Peercoin is based on an August 2012 paper which listed the authors as Scott Nadal and Sunny King. Sunny King, who also created Primecoin, is a pseudonym.[6] Nadal's involvement had diminished by November 2013, leaving King as Peercoin's sole core developer.

Peercoin was inspired by bitcoin, and it shares much of the source code and technical implementation of bitcoin. The Peercoin source code is distributed under the MIT/X11 software license.

Unlike Bitcoin, Namecoin, and Litecoin, Peercoin does not have a hard limit on the number of possible coins, but is designed to eventually attain an annual inflation rate of 1%. There is a deflationary aspect to Peercoin as the transaction fee of 0.01 PPC/kb paid to the network is destroyed. This feature, along with increased energy efficiency, aim to allow for greater long-term scalability.

PotCoin is a peer-to-peer cryptocurrency which exists with the aim of becoming the standard form of payment for the legalized cannabis industry. PotCoin is an open source software project released under the MIT/X11 license and was technically nearly identical to Litecoin until August 23, 2015, when Potcoin changed to POSV similar to Reddcoin.

PotCoin is not managed by any central authority and provides a decentralised solution for the transfer of value. As of August 2014, PotCoin has received mainstream media coverage from agencies such as Fox Business, Vice, and TechCrunch.

Ripple is also known as XRP. XRP is the 2nd largest market cap coin. Eobot has Cloud Mining of BTC that can automatically be converted into XRP. Ripple, or XRP, is a payment protocol that functions as a payment system, currency exchange and a remittance network and works with fiat currencies, cryptocurrencies, and commodities. Ripple uses a shared public ledger like the Bitcoin blockchain and holds balances as well as buy and sell orders, which makes it the first distributed exchange. Changes in the ledger are reached through a process known as consensus. Ripple's infancy began in 2004 with the creation of RipplePay by creator Ryan Fugger.

In 2011, Jed McCaleb conceived of a new system which was to be built by Arthur Britto and David Schwartz. This new system was designed to be faster and use less energy than Bitcoin. From there, the team approached Fugger. After a long term debate with established members of the community, Fugger handed control over to McCaleb and his team. In 2012, OpenCoin, Inc. was formed. OpenCoin began development and received early investments from the likes of Andreessen Horowitz and Google Ventures. This is about the time they began incorporating Bitcoin into the mix, with what they titled the Bitcoin Bridge. It allowed anyone to send a payment in any currency to a Bitcoin address.

Since then, Ripple has been focused on expanding into the banking market. This has been a source of much debate. Ripple is moving more and more into compliance with FinCEN and other regulatory boards. Adding to the debate is the controversy over the security of Ripple's "consensus".

Used by companies such as UniCredit, UBS and Santander, Ripple has been increasingly adopted by banks and payment networks as settlement infrastructure technology, with American Banker explaining that "from banks' perspective, distributed ledgers like the Ripple system have a number of advantages over cryptocurrencies like bitcoin," including price and security.

XEM is the currency of the NEM platform. It is a 100% original codebase coin. It is written in Java and JavaScript with 100% original source code. NEM has a stated goal of a wide distribution model and has introduced new features in blockchain technology in its proof-of-importance (POI) algorithm.

Zcash is a cryptocurrency that grew out of the Zerocoin project, aimed at improving anonymity for Bitcoin users. The Zerocoin protocol was initially improved and transformed into Zerocash, which thus yielded the Zcash cryptocurrency in 2016. The founder and CEO of Zcash is Zooko Wilcox-O'Hearn. Its founding team includes cryptographer Matthew D. Green from Johns Hopkins University.

Zcash payments are published on a public blockchain, but users are able to use an optional privacy feature to conceal the sender, recipient, and amount being transacted. Like Bitcoin, Zcash has a fixed total supply of 21 million units. Zcash affords private transactors the option of "selective disclosure", allowing a user to prove payment for auditing purposes. One such reason is to allow private transactors the choice to comply with anti-money laundering or tax regulations.

On April 4, 2017, Zcash entered the top 10 cryptocurrencies by market cap, but has since retreated to 17th place as of September 2017.

3 HOW I INVESTED

November 2016 was the month when Ethereum was added to the Coinbase app. A year passed since my fail investment in Bitcoin and I was decided to invest a bit more in Ether. It was me who told my brother about it and at that time the price per unit was under £7 .

July 2017

Sold ethereum using EUR Wallet	-10.0000	-£1,629.80
Sold ethereum using EUR Wallet	-10.0000	-£1,569.74

June 2017

Sold ethereum using EUR Wallet	-4.0000	-£844.17
Sold ethereum using GBP Wallet	-6.0000	-£1,016.58

March 2017

Sold ethereum using GBP Wallet	-10.0000	-£371.37

December 2016

Bought ethereum using Visa debit *******1869	13.0000	£80.72

November 2016

Bought ethereum using Visa debit *******1869	15.0000	£102.17
Bought ethereum using Visa debit *******1869		£102.80

By December 2016 I had 40 Ether Coins in my ETH Wallet. I paid £285 for them, about £7.10 per unit and I made a promise to myself that I will keep them until they will hit a value of at least £500. I also told my wife to stop me selling until they will reach a huge value, somewhere close to a thousand pounds.

Off curse I didn't kept my word and in March 2017, I sold 10 ETH for £371 just to be sure I got back to money I invested. I was happy I got amost £100 profit and 30 Ethereum left in my Wallet. Silly me!

I bought 40 with £7 and sold 10 with £37... sounds like a good deal?

After just three months, in June, Ethereum reached a record value of £186 so I decided to sell 10 ETH to secure a huge profit. £1860 landed in my account and paid for a brilliant all-inclusive holiday in Tenerife.

At the beginning of July, Etherem had a huge spike hitting £300.69, but instead of selling at the top and secure another big slice of pie I decided to wait and see. Bad choice again because the Ethereum plunged to half of the spike value. When the value become hectic I decided to cash out and accept the fact that Ethereum was the best investment until now.

Withdrew the last 20 ETH for £3200, adding up the tally to £5533 made with £285 invested at the beginning.

All this transactions occurred between November 2016 and July 2017. It took me just ten months to make a £5246 profit from my gut feeling about Ethereum.

With 1941% profit I can say now that I redeemed myself after the Bitcoin mistake.

Meanwhile, in May 2017, on the Coinbase app was added a new cryptocurrency: Litecoin. This coin was on the market since 2013 and was quite steady around £10 for years.

After May 2017, Litecoin had a spike and the value went up to £21 than slowly went down. I bought just 7 Litecoins at £18.50 per unit because I didn't had the same Ethereum gut feeling about it.

But as all the Cryptocurrencies, the Litecoin went up, reaching a £62 spike in late July. I consider this a small investment and I set my target at £130 per unit, when I will cash out for a 1000% profit.

I did a proper research in mining and faucet websites and I selected few of them for my personal use. For faucet I claim the reward once a day for most websites but some of the website can offer even a 5-minutes claim period, which is great if you spend your day at the computer doing something else. I will explain this in detail in the next chapter.

4 INVESTMENT TIME

Probably by now you are bored with all this stories and you want to know the real stuff.

After months of research and analyses I can say that mining, faucet and investing in low-price cryptocurrency can bring profit.

I kept a close look on the value of cryptocurrencies and made notes about how their value has changed. I did this research to see which cryptocurrency had the biggest raise and to check which one is the most volatile.

The first step in this journey is to create the main wallet and I recommend Coinbase, a digital asset exchange company headquartered in San Francisco, California. It operates exchanges of Ethereum and Litecoin in 32 countries, and Bitcoin transactions and storage in 190 countries worldwide. There are 10.500.00 Coinbase users worldwide and 35.100.00 wallets created in the app.

The Coinbase app will be the base of all transactions and you can deposit and withdraw money anytime for a small fee. Here you can transfer the money from faucet and mining from the other websites and from the Coinbase wallet you can pay for mining or other facilities.

A Coinpot.co account is mandatory for the next steps.

CoinPot is a brand new cryptocurrency microwallet, designed to collect and combine faucet payouts and earnings from a number of different faucets/sources. CoinPot supports multiple currencies: bitcoin, dogecoin and litecoin initially and will consolidate earnings from popular faucets such as Moon Bitcoin, Moon Dogecoin, Moon Litecoin, Bonus Bitcoin and Bit Fun

The Coinpot wallet will show the history of your transactions in graphics, recent transactions and the option to deposit, withdraw and convert Bitcoin, Litecoin and Dogecoin. When made my first withdraw, in Bitcoin and Litecoin and I received the amount in less than a hour.

For faucet I used the five

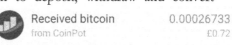

websites mentioned above: Moon Bitcoin, Moon Dogecoin, Moon Litecoin, Bonus Bitcoin and Bit Fun and I will share my knowledge and experience in the Faucet chapter.

For exchange and mining I can say EOBot is the best option because is one of the oldest running cloud service provider on the internet. They offer cryptocurrency mining for SHA256 and Scrypt algorithms that is running on their Antminer S series miner rigs. Their more than 590 000 users can enjoy the benefits of the mining of the digital currencies without the anxiety about the electricity costs or the cooling of the hardware.

Eobot has been founded in 2013 in Los Angeles, California. The owners of the cloud mining service wish to keep their identity securely as there is no About section on their website and they do not share anything about the background of the company.

They offer a daily faucet reward which will give you parts of the crypto currency you have selected. You can switch to Cloud Mining before the faucet and back to the currency after you claimed the reward. This way you will avoid the 5% fee when exchanging currencies for 5 years SHA mining.

Claiming Cloud Mining every day will increase the mining speed and ratio.

Claiming 5 year SHA will bring you profit when the coin you will mine will increase value and adding speed with the daily faucet will maximise the income.

Eobot offers a large range of cryptocurrencies but my advice will be to invest in SHA mining for a low value coin and to hope for the Bitcoin fairy tail to happen again.

I chose to mine Bytecoin because of the ridiculously low value. My current Hashrate is 1.04 GHS which will create approximately 800 Bytecoins each year. The Hashrate will improve daily after each faucet.

5 FAUCET

A faucet is the name given to any website or app which gives away free coins. Each of these websites or apps will give you small amounts of bitcoin for free. Occasionally you need complete simple tasks or play games. Most (if not all) of these sites require you to type a CAPTCHA code every time you use them. The payment delivery time varies from faucet to faucet, from daily to weekly to monthly. Also, some faucets establish a daily limit of use.

I selected seven websites which I use daily and each one is having some great features.

Before I start with the websites and creating accounts, you will need to create a E-Wallet were the faucet rewards will accumulate until you wish to withdraw or transfer. For this task I used COINPOT.

Moonbit.co.in will let you claim satoshi every five minutes but it accumulates until you claim again.

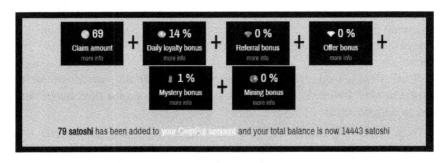

Claim Time	Payout
5 minutes	10 satoshi
10 minutes	18 satoshi
15 minutes	25 satoshi
30 minutes	37 satoshi
1 hour	54 satoshi
4 hours	98 satoshi
1 day	172 satoshi
4 days	245 satoshi
1 week	279 satoshi
4 weeks	369 satoshi

You will earn a % bonus which builds up for every consecutive day that you make at least one faucet claim.

This bonus increases by 1% per day, up to a maximum of 100%

However if you miss a day then your bonus will reset back to 0% and you must build it up again.

Refer your friends to Moon Bitcoin and receive a massive 50% lifetime commission on all their faucet claims. All commission payments are paid instantly in your CoinPot account.

You can boost your faucet earnings even more by completing offers and surveys from any of our offer walls. For every offer/survey completed within the last 30 days you will receive a 5% bonus added on to every faucet claim that you make, up to a maximum of 100%. This is in addition to the amount that you will earn immediately just for completing the offer/survey. The mystery bonus is a random bonus which you will receive for each claim.

When you tick the *Run mining bonus* checkbox they will run a background POW mining process in your browser. Later when you make a faucet claim they will calculate an extra bonus of up to 100% on your faucet claim. The bonus amount is based on how much hashing power you have contributed while the mining process was running, so to maximize your bonus you must leave the Moon Bitcoin tab open in between claims.

PLEASE NOTE: This mining process will increase the CPU usage on your PC/device whilst it is running by 10-80% (depending on the selected CPU usage option). The mining bonus is completely optional so if it causes a problem for you then please turn it off by unticking the *Run mining bonus* checkbox.

Moonliteco.in will let you claim litoshi every five minutes but it accumulates until you claim again.

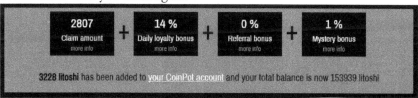

You will earn a % bonus which builds up for every consecutive day that you make at least one faucet claim.

This bonus increases by 1% per day, up to a maximum of 100%

However if you miss a day then your bonus will reset back to 0% and you must build it up again.

Refer your friends to Moon Litecoin and receive a massive 50% lifetime commission on all their faucet claims. All commission payments are paid instantly in your CoinPot account.

The mystery bonus is a random bonus which you will receive for each claim.

Dogeco.in will let you claim dogecoin every five minutes but it accumulates until you claim again.

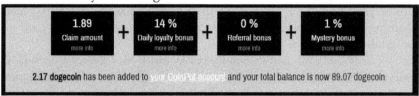

You will earn a % bonus which builds up for every consecutive day that you make at least one faucet claim.

This bonus increases by 1% per day, up to a maximum of 100%

However if you miss a day then your bonus will reset back to 0% and you must build it up again.

Refer your friends to Moon Dogecoin and receive a massive 50% lifetime commission on all their faucet claims. All commission payments are paid instantly in your CoinPot account.

The mystery bonus is a random bonus which you will receive for each claim.

Bitfun.co will let you claim satoshi every three minutes. You can multiply your earnings by playing Dice Game or earn more by completing offers and surveys.

Refer your friends to Bitfun and receive a massive 50% lifetime commission on all their faucet claims. All commission payments are paid instantly in your CoinPot account.

Bonusbitcoin.co will let you can claim up to 5,000 satoshi every 15 minutes. The current average is 100 satoshi. Simply complete the captcha and then click on the Claim now button.

They will pay out a 5% daily bonus for your total amount and you can multiply your earnings by playing Dice Game or earn even more by completing Offers and Surveys

Refer your friends to BonusBitcoin and receive a massive 50% lifetime commission on all their faucet claims. All commission payments are paid instantly in your CoinPot account.

Freebitco.in will let you roll each hour for a payout in Bitcoin.

$$0 - 9885 = 0.00000056 \text{ BTC}$$
$$9886 - 9985 = 0.00000555 \text{ BTC}$$
$$9986 - 9993 = 0.00005552 \text{ BTC}$$
$$9994 - 9997 = 0.00055521 \text{ BTC}$$
$$9998 - 9999 = 0.00555207 \text{ BTC}$$
$$10000 = 0.05552070 \text{ BTC}$$

I never rolled more than 9885 until now so my payout was always the lowest. Any earning from this website will not be transferred automatically to the Coinpot wallet.

You can earn 4.08 % annual interest on your Freebitcoin balance. All you need to do is to maintain a balance of at least 30.000 satoshi in the account and you will be paid interest every day. There is no lock-in period to earn interest and your balance can be withdrawn for a small fee. To start a withdraw process you need to have at least 0.00030000 Bitcoin, 30.000 satoshi, in your account.

Freedoge.co.in will let you roll each hour for Dogecoins, similar to the Freebitcoin website. See the attached table for details.

LUCKY NUMBER	PAYOUT
0 - 9885	1.04 DOGE
9886 - 9985	20.74 DOGE
9986 - 9993	207.36 DOGE
9994 - 9997	2,073.56 DOGE
9998 - 9999	20,735.65 DOGE
10000	207,356.45 DOGE

I rolled more than 9885 twice, winning 16 dogecoins. The value will be different and is related to the Dogecoin value when the roll is taking place.

LUCKY NUMBER	PAYOUT
0 - 9885	0.78 DOGE
9886 - 9985	15.57 DOGE
9986 - 9993	155.69 DOGE
9994 - 9997	1,556.91 DOGE
9998 - 9999	15,569.08 DOGE
10000	155,690.78 DOGE

09969

You win 16.41 DOGE!

☐ Play sound when timer runs out (TEST SOUND)

Any earning

from this website will not be transferred automatically to the Coinpot wallet. To start a withdraw process you need to have at least 200 Dogecoins in your account and the fee for the transaction will be 1 Dogecoin.

6 MINING

In cryptocurrency a miner is a computer or group of computers 'searching' for cryptocurrency. They constantly verify transactions and as a incentive they get rewarded with cryptocurrency. The first and most well know cryptocurrency is bitcoin.

New units of currency are generated by "mining." This is a computationally intensive task, and it requires a lot of processing power. Essentially, the computer is rewarded for solving difficult math problems. This processing power is used to verify transactions, so all that number-crunching is required for the cryptocurrency to work.

Mining programs tap into your computer's hardware resources and put them to work mining Bitcoin, Litecoin, or another type of cryptocurrency.

Today, there is very much a digital gold rush where people can make a small profit by investing a few hundred dollars in equipment, and then spend months mining for digital coins before any return on their investment sets in.

Litecoins, Dogecoins, and Feathercoins are three Scrypt-based cryptocurrencies that are the best cost-benefit for beginners. At the current value of Litecoins, a person might earn anywhere from 50 cents to 10 dollars per day using consumer level mining hardware. Dogecoins and Feathercoins will yield slightly less profit with the same mining hardware but are becoming more popular daily.

Is It Worth It to Mine Cryptocoins? As a hobby venture, yes, cryptocoin mining can generate a small income of perhaps a dollar or two per day. In particular, Litecoins, Dogecoins, and Feathercoins are very accessible for regular people to mine, and a person can recoup $1000 in hardware costs in about 18-24 months.

As a second income, no, cryptocoin mining is not a reliable way to make substantial money for most people. The profit from mining cryptocoins only becomes significant when someone is willing to invest $3000-$5000 in up-front hardware costs, at which time you could potentially earn $50 per day or more.

Now, there is a small chance that Litecoins, Dogecoins, or Feathercoins will jump in value alongside Bitcoin at some point. Then, possibly, you could find yourself sitting on thousands of dollars in cryptocoins.

If you do decide to try cryptocoin mining, definitely do so as a hobby with a very small income return. Think of it as 'gathering gold dust' instead of collecting actual gold nuggets.

If your objective is to earn substantial money as a second income, then you are better off purchasing cryptocoins with cash instead of mining them, and then tucking them away in the hopes that they will jump in value like gold or silver bullion. If your objective is to make a few digital bucks and spend them somehow, then you just might have a slow way to do that with mining.

Unless you are willing to spend tens of thousands of dollars on industrial hardware and rent an air-conditioned office to house your hardware, there is no profit in mining Bitcoins. You are better off purchasing cryptocurrency with your regular money, and tucking it away in the hopes it will further climb in value.

Litecoins and Dogecoins are the popular digital currencies that are still within the grasp of consumer-level users with hobby budgets, with Feathercoins being a third option that is gaining traction.

For mining and exchange I use EOBOT, a site which serve to mine bitcoins or other crypto-currency that can use the CPU or GPU of your PC. This site is a great solution easy of use wich allow conversion between different crypto-currency and immediately send PayPal payments. You can use as many computers as you want but you can also pay and "rent line" for mining so the mining will be done from somewhere else on your behalf.

For mining I use EOBOT and TELCOMINER.

You know already that EOBOT offers cryptocurrency mining for SHA256 and Scrypt algorithms that is running on their Antminer S series miner rigs. Their more than 590 000 users can enjoy the benefits of the mining of the digital currencies without the anxiety about the electricity costs or the cooling of the hardware.

You can deposit in the account or transfer money from the Coinbase app. For the best result you can invest in Cloud SHA 5 year rental and all the details will be listed when you press the calculate button. The mining will run and create the current selected coin. If you change it than you will start mining the new selection. You can top up the SHA speed any time and as a little bonus change to Cloud Mining before you claim your faucet reward and back to a cryptocurrency after. You will also avoid paying a fee when exchanging currencies from faucet for Cloud SHA speed.

TELCOMINER is a growing Bitcoin cloud mining company with almost 100.000 registered users. TELCOMINER is a trusted miner since 2013, providing efficient, safe and profitable mining which runs on green energy. They have five Data Center Worldwide and when you will open the account you will receive 15 bonus KH/s.
The cloud mining speed is for life and the daily profit is equal to 1.09% of the investment. You can boost your speed anytime.

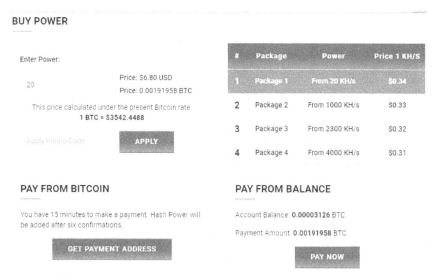

I wish you all the best when investing in cryptocurrencies and I hope my experience will help you in this new path.

6 VOCABULARY

51% attack This occurs when more than half the computing power on a digital currency network is run by a single miner, which theoretically makes them the main controller and authority of that network.

Altcoin The alternatives and rivals to Bitcoin are collectively known as Altcoins. Bitcoin Whitepaper Written by Satoshi Nakamoto in 2008, the famous document explains the Bitcoin concept and protocol. The Bitcoin code was released the following year.

Blockchain is a continuously growing list of records, called blocks, which are linked and secured using cryptography. Each block contains typically a hash pointer as a link to a previous block, a timestamp and transaction data. By design, blockchains are inherently resistant to modification of the data. A blockchain is "an open, distributed ledger that can record transactions between two parties efficiently and in a verifiable and permanent way."

Block reward The recompense a miner receives when they have successfully hashed a transaction block. It can be a mixture of coins and transaction fees.

BOINC Credit System (Berkeley Open Infrastructure for Network Computing) helps volunteers keep track of how much CPU time they have donated to various distributed computing projects. The credit system is designed to eliminate cheating by validating results before granting credit on projects. This ensures users are returning accurate results for both scientific and statistical reasons.

CAPTCHA (a backronym for "Completely Automated Public Turing test to tell Computers and Humans Apart") is a type of challenge-response test used in computing to determine whether or not the user is human.

Cryptocurrency (or **crypto currency**) is a digital asset designed to work as a medium of exchange using cryptographyto secure the transactions and to control the creation of additional units of the currency. Cryptocurrencies are classified as a subset of digital currencies and are also classified as a subset of alternative currencies and virtual currencies

Distributed Ledger is a database that is consensually shared and synchronized across network spread across multiple sites, institutions or geographies. It allows transactions to have public "witnesses," thereby making a cyberattack more difficult. The participant at each node of the network can access the recordings shared across that network and can own an identical copy of it. Further, any changes or additions made to the ledger are reflected and copied to all participants in a matter of seconds or minutes. Underlying the distributed ledger technology is the blockchain, which is the technology that underlies bitcoin.

Faucets are a reward system, in the form of a website or app, that dispenses rewards in the form of a satoshi, which is a hundredth of a millionth BTC, for visitors to claim in exchange for completing a captcha or task as described by the website. There are also faucets that dispense alternative cryptocurrencies. A number of coins are given away for free to generate interest and build initial momentum in a cryptocurrency mining community.

Fiat currency Currency that a government has declared to be legal tender, but it is not backed by a physical commodity.

Fork The emergence or creation of a new version of a particular blockchain. It typically happens when one set of miners begins hashing a different set of transaction blocks from another.

Genesis block If you know your biblical readings you'll get know why this is the term for the very first block in the block chain

Hash Rate is the output of a hash function and, as it relates to cryptocurrencies, the Hash Rate is the speed at which a compute is completing an operation in the cryptocurrencies code. A higher hash rate is better when mining as it increases your opportunity of finding the next block and receiving the reward.

JavaScript is an object-oriented computer programming language commonly used to create interactive effects within web browsers.

Llitoshi is 0.00000001 of a litecoin. It is the bitcoin equivalent of a satoshi.

Mining is the process by which transactions are verified and added to the public ledger, known as the block chain, and also the means through which new bitcoin are released. Anyone with access to the internet and suitable hardware can participate in mining.

Satoshi is the smallest fraction of a Bitcoin that can currently be sent: 0.00000001 BTC, that is, a hundredth of a millionth BTC. In the future, however, the protocol may be updated to allow further subdivisions, should they be needed

Scrypt is a password-based key derivation function created by Colin Percival, originally for the Tarsnap online backup service. The algorithm was specifically designed to make it costly to perform large-scale custom hardware attacks by requiring large amounts of memory. In 2016, the scrypt algorithm was published by IETF as RFC 7914. A simplified version of scrypt is used as a proof-of-work scheme by a number of cryptocurrencies, first implemented by an anonymous programmer called ArtForz in Tenebrix and followed by Fairbrix and Litecoin soon after.

SHA-2 is a set of cryptographic hash functions designed by the United States National Security Agency (NSA). Cryptographic hash functions are mathematical operations run on digital data, by comparing the computed "hash" to a known and expected hash value, a person can determine the data's integrity. For example, computing the hash of a downloaded file and comparing the result to a previously published hash result can show whether the download has been modified or tampered with. A key aspect of cryptographic hash functions is their collision resistance: nobody should be able to find two different input values that result in the same hash output.

Silk Road The controversial underground online marketplace, which has been often linked to cryptocurrencies in the past, was shut down by the FBI in 2013.

ABOUT THE AUTHOR

I am a Romanian writer, born 04/06/1986, living in the United Kingdom, since 2010. Husband of Raluca, father of Dennis.
With a Bachelor Degree in Physical Education and Sports and a PhD in Sports, experience in Teaching, coaching, healthcare and investments I can say I am a Jack off all trades.

www.ingramcontent.com/pod-product-compliance
Lightning Source LLC
Chambersburg PA
CBHW070904070326
40690CB00009B/1989